Animal Icons
COYOTES

Sheila Griffin Llanas

ABDO Publishing Company

CHECKERBOARD ANIMAL LIBRARY

ANIMAL ICONS

visit us at
www.abdopublishing.com

Published by ABDO Publishing Company, PO Box 398166, Minneapolis, MN 55439.
Copyright © 2013 by Abdo Consulting Group, Inc. International copyrights reserved in all countries.
No part of this book may be reproduced in any form without written permission from the publisher.
The Checkerboard Library™ is a trademark and logo of ABDO Publishing Company.

Printed in the United States of America, North Mankato, Minnesota.
112012
012013

 PRINTED ON RECYCLED PAPER

Cover Photo: Getty Images
Interior Photos: Alamy pp. 4–5, 8, 10–11, 22–23; Animals Animals p. 27; Corbis pp. 1, 14–15,
    20–21, 28–29; Getty Images pp. 10, 26; iStockphoto pp. 9, 16–17, 18–19, 27; Konrad Wothe/
    Minden Pictures/National Geographic Stock pp. 12–13; Michael Melford/National Geographic
    Stock pp. 6–7; Sumio Harada/Minden Pictures/National Geographic Stock p. 17

Editors: Tamara L. Britton, Megan M. Gunderson, Stephanie Hedlund
Art Direction: Neil Klinepier

Cataloging-in-Publication Data

Llanas, Sheila Griffin, 1958-
 Coyotes / Sheila Griffin Llanas.
   p. cm. -- (Animal icons)
Includes bibliographical references and index.
ISBN 978-1-61783-570-4
1. Coyote--Juvenile literature.   I. Title.
599.74--dc22

                                          2012946537

CONTENTS

COYOTES

On a South Dakota prairie, a lone coyote hunts **rodents** in the tall grass. It trots in circles and sniffs. It arcs its back and pounces. It wags its bushy tail.

The coyote looks like a dog. That's because coyotes are dogs! They are part of the family **Canidae**. Coyotes have been called American jackals, prairie wolves, and song dogs.

Coyotes live in mountains, forests, plains, and deserts. They **inhabit** every state in Mexico. They live in all of the United States but Hawaii. Their range also covers most of Canada.

As you can see, coyotes have spread far and wide. They are survivors. Many people consider coyotes to be nothing but pesky predators. But in some **cultures**, they are respected teachers that are smart and magical. Whether friend or foe, coyotes are an animal icon.

An icon is a cultural symbol. Animal icons stand for the people and land of nations, states, and cities. Animal icons are shown on flags and signs. They appear in songs, legends, and stories. They represent history. They teach people about nature and about themselves.

COYOTE HISTORY

The oldest fossilized coyote bones were dug up in the New Mexico desert. They proved coyotes have been around since the Pleistocene epoch. That was 2.6 million to 11,700 years ago!

By the 1800s, coyotes lived between the Rocky Mountains and the Mississippi River. Predators such as wolves and mountain lions kept the coyote population balanced.

When pioneers settled in the West, coyotes saw their livestock as food. Coyotes ate sheep, pigs, and chickens. Farmers saw coyotes as pests. They killed the coyotes with poisoned meat.

Fur trappers caught muskrats, foxes, skunks, and coyotes for their valuable fur. As the stories go, the coyotes ate the bait without getting caught in the traps! Is this frontier lore fact or fiction? One thing is certain. Efforts to get rid of coyotes have backfired.

Coyotes have lived in Florida since the 1960s, when they migrated from Georgia and Alabama.

Nonetheless, by the early 1900s, more than 1 million coyotes had been killed. Ranchers, trappers, hunters, and park rangers had poisoned, trapped, and shot them.

Unlike other mammals that lost **habitat**, coyotes gained ground. Canadian coyotes **migrated** into the northeastern United States. In the 1940s, the coyote's range expanded east of the Mississippi River. The last state they reached was Delaware, in 1993.

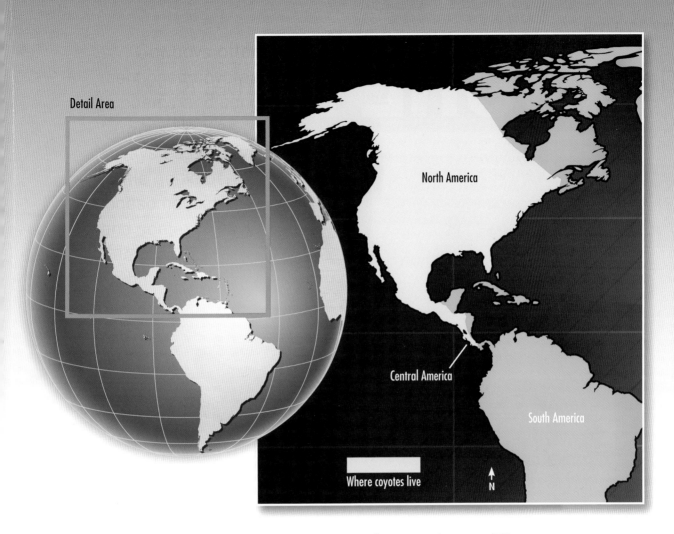

Detail Area

North America

Central America

South America

Where coyotes live

N

Today, coyotes almost cover the continent. They are still one of the most hunted animals in the United States. But it will take more than poison, guns, and traps to stop the wily coyote!

MORE LORE

Coyote is a famous Trickster in North American native **cultures**. In the traditions of many native peoples, the Trickster is a folk hero. He represents a society's fears, failures, and ideals. He explains how things came to be.

To the Mayans, Coyote represented Earth. They believed the god Quetzalcoatl emerged from its jaws.

In Native American mythology, the Trickster was part coyote, part human, and part magic! He was a healer and an inventor. He plotted to foil others to get what he wanted. Tales of his actions combined lessons about morality with humor.

Aztec people told stories of Old Man Coyote. He brought music and

The name coyote is from the
Aztec word Coyotl.

Though it is not a beautiful blue, the coyote's dirt-colored fur is thick and warm. Today, a trapper can earn $50 for a quality pelt.

laughter into the world. However, he could also bring mischief and misfortune.

In a tale told by the Pima, a brown bird once bathed in a lake. It became the Bluebird. Coyote wanted to be blue, too. So, he also bathed in the lake. His fur turned blue! Coyote pranced around, showing off his new color.

As he pranced, Coyote did not watch where he was going. He crashed into a tree and fell to the ground. His fur turned the color of dirt. He has been that color ever since.

In a Zuni tale, Coyote wanted to fly. So, he begged Crows to help him. Crows stuck feathers in Coyote's fur. Coyote bragged about his bird skills. But Coyote sang off-key. And, he danced out of step.

Crows ignored him until Coyote tried to boss them around! Then, Crows helped Coyote fly high in the sky. In midair, they took back their feathers! Coyote fell to the ground so fast that his tail caught on fire. To this day, Coyote's tail has a black tip.

NOSE TO TAIL

As the Pima Native Americans noted in their Trickster tale, coyotes are earth-colored. Their fur is brown, red, black, gray, or creamy white. And the Zuni were also correct. The tips of their tails are always black!

Western coyotes weigh 20 to 50 pounds (9 to 23 kg). Eastern coyotes are larger, weighing in at 50 to 60 pounds (23 to 27 kg). Why this difference? Well, where food is more plentiful, coyotes grow larger.

From nose to tail, coyotes measure 3 to 4 feet (1 to 1.25 m) long. They stand 15 to 20 inches (38 to 51 cm) tall at the shoulder. Females are smaller than males.

As predators, coyotes have special skills. They have sharp senses of hearing, sight, and smell. And, they can run 35 miles per hour (56 km/h)!

Their bodies have other useful tools for hunting. Musk glands leave a scent when they urinate or defecate. A coyote that sniffs an area and urinates a few drops is marking its territory. The mark tells other predators to stay away!

COYOTE TAXONOMY

Kingdom: Animalia
Phylum: Chordata
Class: Mammalia
Order: Carnivora
Family: Canidae
Genus: Canis
Species: Canis latrans

WHAT'S FOR DINNER?

The coyote is a carnivore. Small **game** such as gophers, voles, and chipmunks are easy prey. So are squirrels, rabbits, and raccoons. Coyotes also eat ducks and turkeys. They even eat insects and lizards!

However, the coyote's diet includes more than meat. Coyotes munch on blueberries and raspberries. Apples and pears that have fallen from trees make tasty meals. Coyotes also raid farm fields for market crops such as melons.

In winter, coyotes can feast on large game. Why? In harsh weather, old or sick animals can't keep up with their herds. Coyotes look for these lone animals. Hunting in pairs or packs, the coyotes take turns chasing their prey. When it gets tired, the coyotes move in for the kill.

Coyotes also **scavenge** for food. They follow packs of wolves that are hunting. When wolves make a kill and finish eating, coyotes move in and eat the leftovers. They also eat **carrion**.

Coyotes hunt large prey in packs. They attack from behind and pull the animal to the ground.

Coyotes hunt rodents alone. They listen for their prey under the snow and then pounce on it.

When hungry, **urban** coyotes take advantage of their location. If they live near a farm, they will eat poultry, sheep, and pigs. In cities, they will raid garbage cans and vegetable gardens. Pet food left for outdoor pets is always an easy meal.

COYOTE BEHAVIOR

Coyotes are smart. They are known for their **cunning** and swiftness. They have long been hunted for preying on livestock and raiding crops. So their ability to adapt is one of their greatest skills.

Western coyotes live where there is more open land and fewer people. So their packs are larger than eastern packs. However, there is less food available in desert **environments**. So western coyotes are smaller than eastern coyotes.

Eastern coyotes have less land to roam. But they live where the human population is greater. So there is more food available.

Coyotes prefer to live alone. But they will form packs to secure a home range. The range can be as small as 4 or as big as 15 square miles (10 to 39 sq km). Pack members mark its borders with their scent. They patrol the hunting grounds and keep strange coyotes out.

Coyotes communicate using 11 different sounds.

Coyotes usually respect another pack's borders. They will walk out of their way to avoid cutting through another pack's home range. Taking the long way is safer. It is part of a coyote's adaptability.

Coyotes make themselves comfortable in prairie, forest, desert, mountain, and tropical environments.

19

BIRTH TO DEATH

Coyotes tightly guard the innermost part of their home range. This area has the best food and the best sleeping spots. Coyotes sleep out in the open. They only use dens to raise pups.

When courting a female, males do not fight each other. Instead, they try to impress the female. The female makes the final choice. A new coyote couple is very playful. They wrestle and nibble each other. Between January and March, they mate.

Coyote couples build their underground dens in hidden areas safe from predators. Sandy hillsides or steep creek banks make good spots. **Urban** coyotes make dens in storm drains, storage sheds, vacant lots, city parks, or golf courses. Any dry, safe place will do.

Mother coyotes are **pregnant** for about 65 days. The average **litter** size is four to seven pups. Each tiny pup is blind, helpless, and weighs only half a pound (0.25 kg).

A coyote couple will stay together for many years, sometimes for life.

By drinking their mother's milk, coyote pups triple in size during their first two weeks of life.

When pups lick an adult's lips to stimulate vomiting, this is called "licking up."

Only the female and her pups live in the den. The male sleeps outside. He hunts and brings food back to the den in his stomach. When the pups lick his lips, he **vomits** the food so they can eat.

When the pups are two to three weeks old, they emerge from their den. Then, both parents can hunt for food. The pups learn to hunt by imitating their parents. They practice their skills by hunting gophers, voles, and mice.

Chances are about half the pups will not survive to adulthood. Besides disease and hunger, pups have predators. Eagles and owls can easily carry off a pup in their talons. Bobcats, lynxes, mountain lions, and wolves catch them for a snack. Even a rattlesnake will eat a pup.

In late summer or early fall, the pups are grown. One or two will stay in their parents' pack. The parents chase away the other pups. These pups go off to live on their own. They will find mates and have their own pups. Coyotes live for six to eight years in the wild.

THE ICONIC COYOTE

The Trickster of Native American lore is part of the wider **culture**. The coyote's scientific name, *Canis latrans*, means "barking dog." Its yips and cries are the soundtrack of the Wild West.

Cattle ranchers heard coyotes howl at sunrise and sunset. To some, the sound was happy. To others, it was sad.

The Call of the Plains

"I dream of the wide, wide prairies
Touched with their glistening sheen,
The coyotes' cry and the wind-swept sky
And the waving billows of green!"

Cowboys often mentioned coyotes in poems and songs. Cowboy life was not always easy. Driving cattle could be lonesome, dangerous, and sometimes boring. A lonely cowboy might be happy just to see a coyote!

A Nevada Cowpuncher to His Beloved

"Perhaps a gaunt coyote
Will go a-lopin' by
An' linger on the
mountain ridge
An' cock his wary eye."

The coyote would work its way from the Wild West to popular **culture**. In 1949, cartoon character Wile E. Coyote started trying to catch the Road Runner. Like the Trickster, he is always foiled by his own tricks.

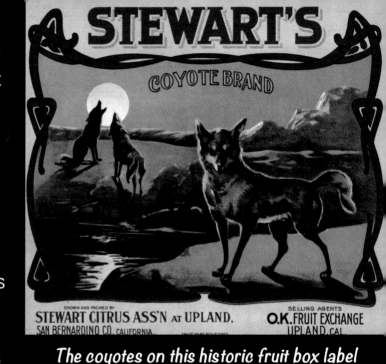

The coyotes on this historic fruit box label indicated the fruit was from California, not from an eastern citrus-producing state such as Florida.

Many states have named things after the coyote. Since 1949, the coyote has been South Dakota's official state animal. And, South Dakota is nicknamed the Coyote State.

The coyote is Arizona's unofficial mascot. The Phoenix Coyotes are the state's professional hockey team. In New Mexico, visitors enjoy Coyote Creek state park. Californians enjoy winter sports at Coyote SNO-PARK.

Today, Wile E. Coyote is still trying to catch the Road Runner!

INTO THE FUTURE

In 1997, a coyote dashed into a building in Seattle, Washington. It scurried through the lobby and bolted into an elevator. In 2002, a coyote boarded a train in Portland, Oregon. It curled up on a seat, ready for the trip. In 2007, a coyote wandered into a Chicago, Illinois, sandwich shop. He slipped into an open cooler.

In these cases, animal control officers safely captured the coyotes and released them outside. But some people wondered, are coyotes a pest or a treasure? Do they help or harm communities and nature?

Some people view **urban** coyotes as a big problem. They argue that these coyotes kill pet dogs and cats. Sometimes, coyotes bite people.

Others see coyotes as helpful. Coyotes control **rodent** and Canada geese populations. They drag away roadkill as large as deer.

Today, there are more coyotes than at any other time in history.

Even so, some city governments kill or relocate **urban** coyotes. Since 2000, nearly 1 million coyotes have been killed by the US Department of Agriculture's Wildlife Services. But as history has shown, trying to get rid of coyotes does not work. Coyotes from outside the area will soon move in.

Coyotes are smart, resourceful, and adapt well to changing situations. They have **migrated** across the continent. Throughout history, they have appeared in Native American mythology, cowboy songs, and television cartoons. Love them or hate them, the coyote is an animal icon.

GLOSSARY

Canidae (KAN-uh-dee) - the scientific Latin name for the dog family. Members of this family are called canids. They include wolves, jackals, foxes, coyotes, and domestic dogs.

carrion - dead, rotting flesh.

culture - the customs, arts, and tools of a nation or a people at a certain time.

cunning - getting what is wanted in a clever and sometimes deceptive way.

environment - all the surroundings that affect the growth and well-being of a living thing.

game - wild animals hunted for food or sport.

habitat - a place where a living thing is naturally found.

inhabit - to live in or occupy a place. If a place is not lived in, it is uninhabited.

litter - all of the pups born at one time to a mother coyote.

migrate - to move from one place to another, often to find food.

pregnant - having one or more babies growing within the body.

rodent - any of several related animals that have large front teeth for gnawing. Common rodents include mice, squirrels, and beavers.

scavenge - to search through waste for something that can be used.

urban - of or relating to a city.

vomit - the act of rejecting the contents of the stomach out through the mouth.

WEB SITES

To learn more about coyotes, visit ABDO Publishing Company online. Web sites about coyotes are featured on our Book Links page. These links are routinely monitored and updated to provide the most current information available.

www.abdopublishing.com

INDEX